A BATHROOM BOOK
FOR PEOPLE

not pooping or peeing but

USING THE BATHROOM
AS AN ESCAPE

A BATHROOM BOOK FOR PEOPLE

not pooping or peeing but

USING THE BATHROOM AS AN ESCAPE

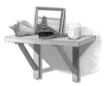

JOE PERA

Illustrated by

JOE BENNETT

A Tom Doherty Associates Book
New York

Are you alright?

You are now.

You're in the bathroom.

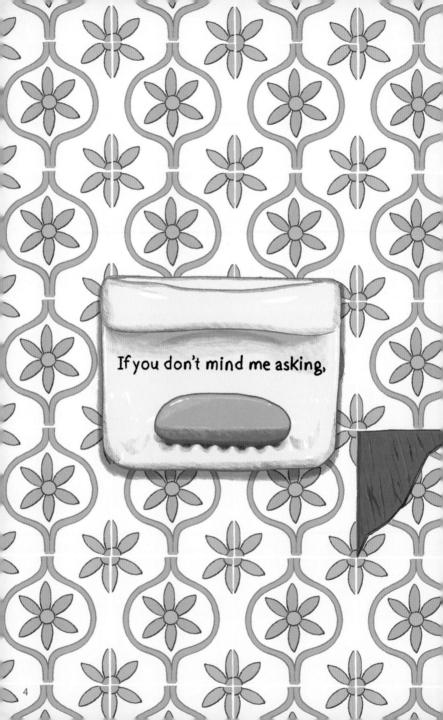

If you don't mind me asking,

what's going on?

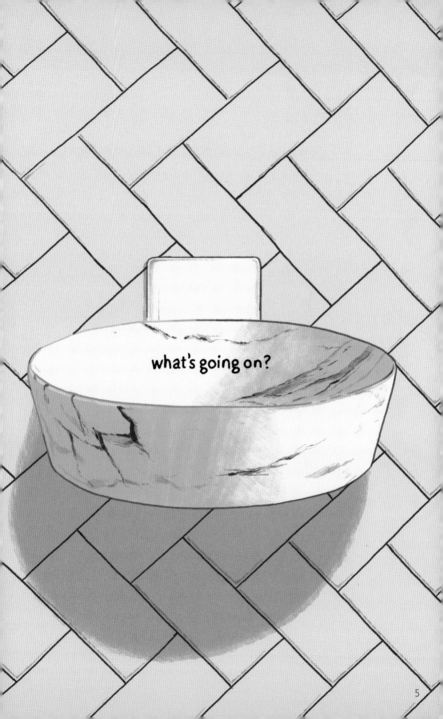

Did you just excuse yourself to do a toot?

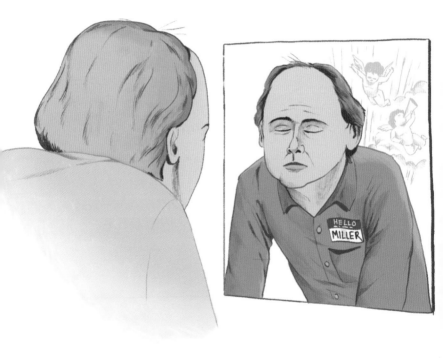

Are you hiding away from your kids?

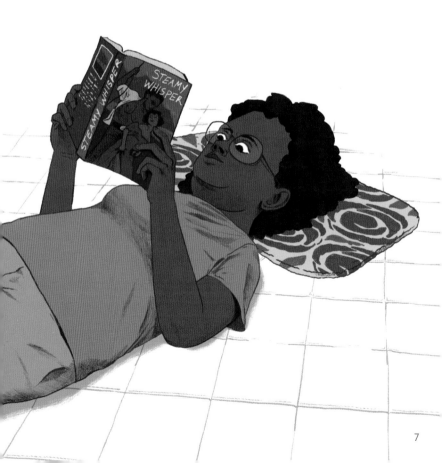

Or is your date going great and you are taking a moment to appreciate it before it inevitably falls apart?

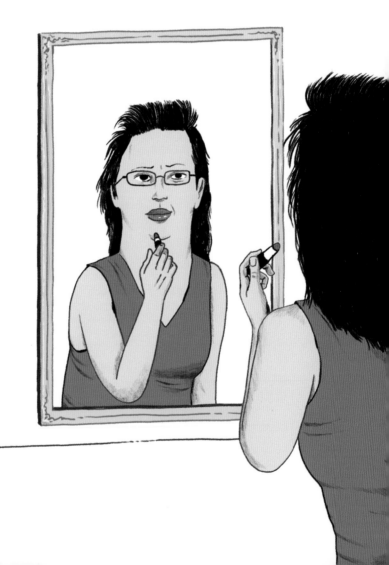

Are you working up the confidence
to say "no" to a car salesman?

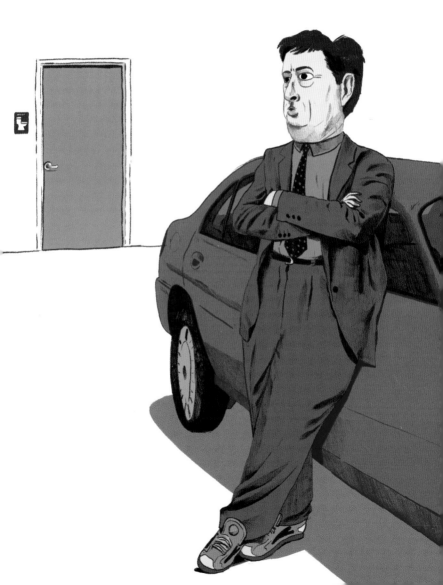

Trying to think of something to say
that'll change the judge's mind?

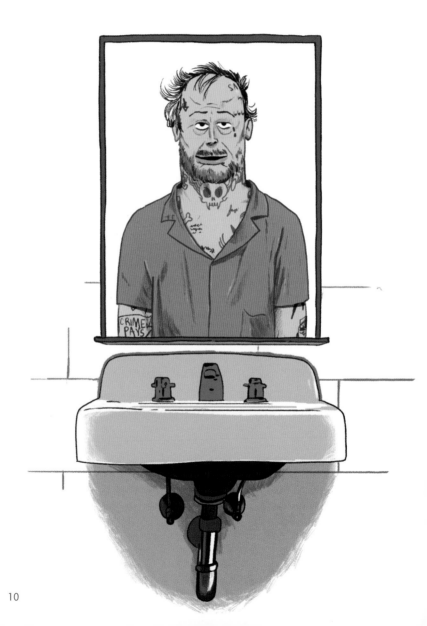

Or, like me, are you flushing an engagement ring down the toilet for the third time this year?

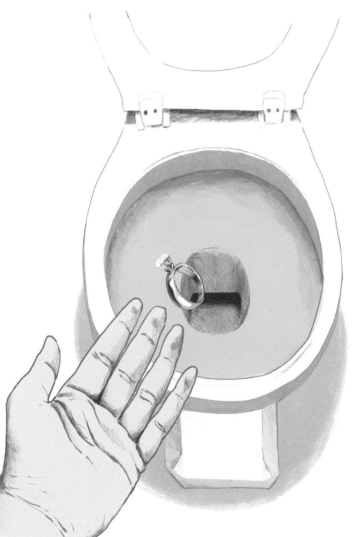

I cannot be tied down.

Whatever it is, you can relax.

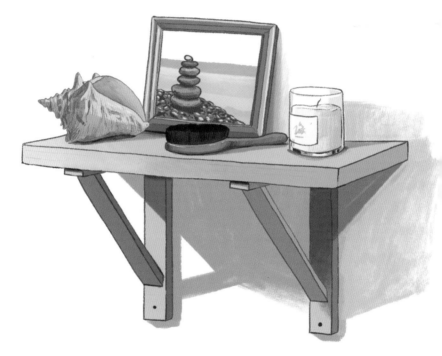

Because here, in the bathroom, you are safe and alone...

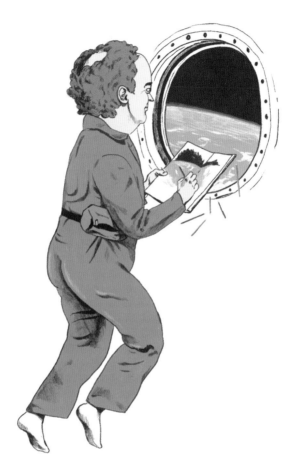

...the only astronaut awake
on the International Space Station...

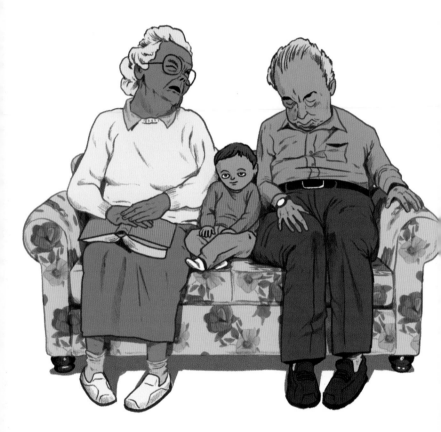

...between two sleeping grandparents
watching the Golf Channel on mute...

...looking out at the lake on a snowy night that's not too cold. And it's quiet too because everyone else is back in town celebrating New Year's Eve.

But you wouldn't trade 100 midnight kisses for the peace and calm you've got right now, on the shore of Lake Ontario.

15

One thing that helps me calm down is to repeat the word "Hawaii" over and over.

Feel free to try it.

Hawaii.

Hawaii.

Hawaii.

Hawaii.

Hawaii.

I've never been there myself but I heard it's nice.

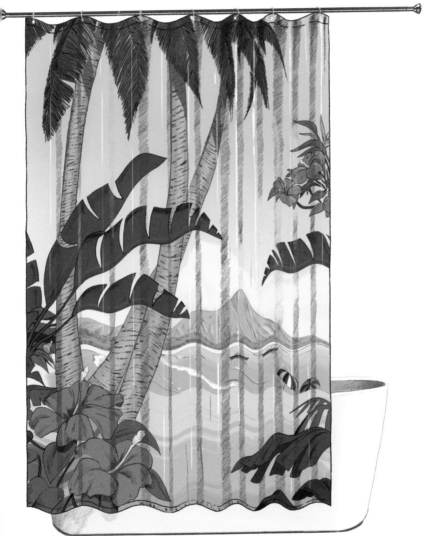

You could say, "Tampa, Tampa," but it's not quite the same cause in Hawaii, there are pineapples.

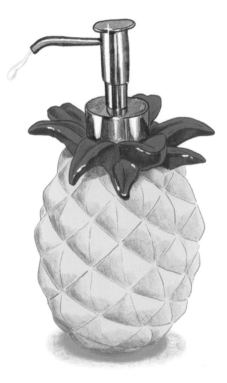

Because it grows in tropical places and takes three years to mature,
pineapple's not the most affordable fruit but in my opinion,
one of the best.

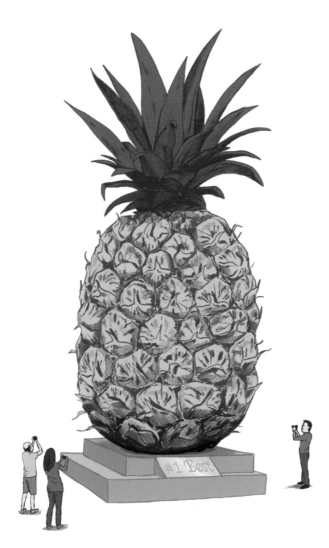

I don't have refined taste buds -
my favorite flavor is salt & pepper -
but a lot of other people agree as well.

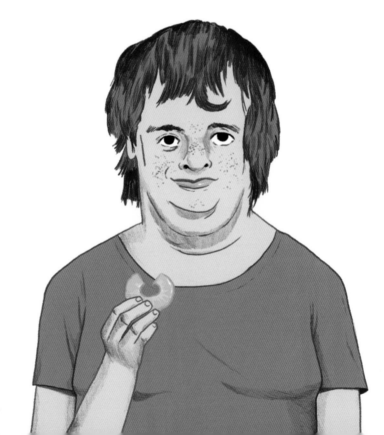

Did you know that on the island of Oahu
they even make pineapple wine?

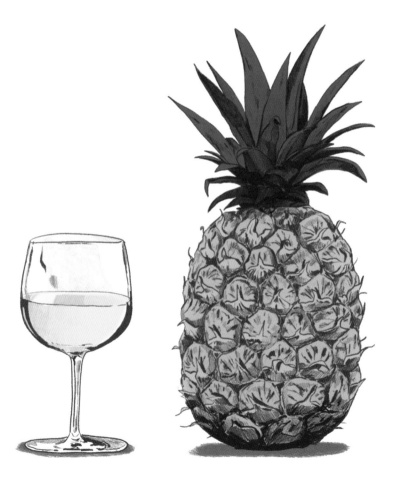

Wow.

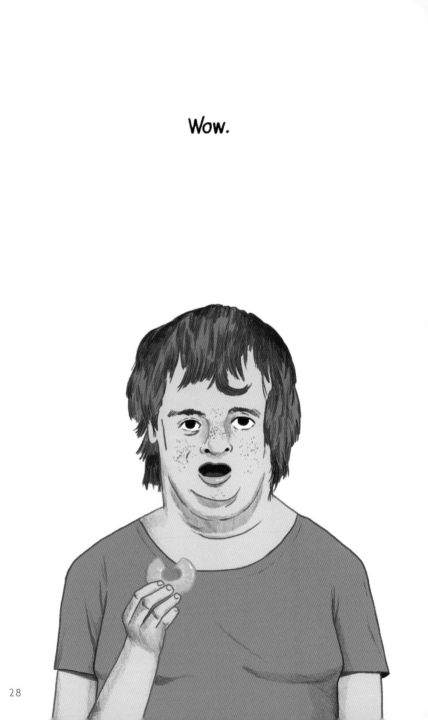

If you want to pretend you're near a Hawaiian waterfall, just turn on the shower or bath a little.

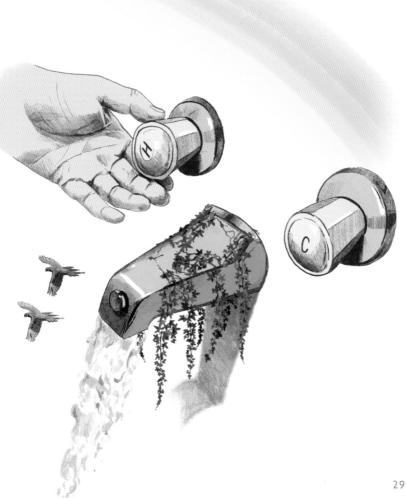

No one will know. They will just think you are
washing your hands for a long time.

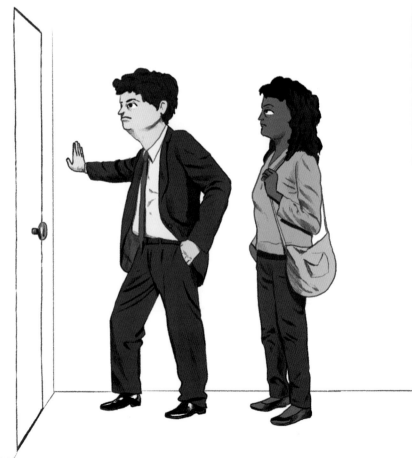

Close your eyes and listen...

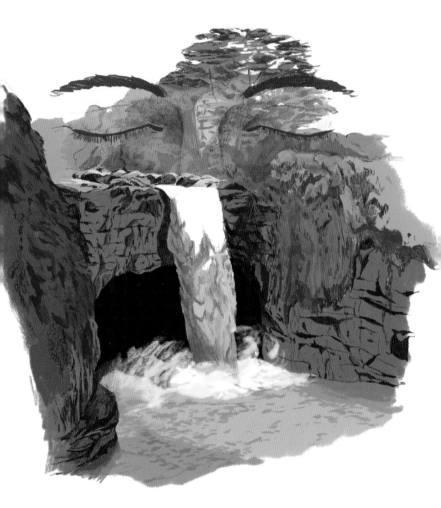

can you hear the waterfalls?

Wind blowing through the kukui trees*?

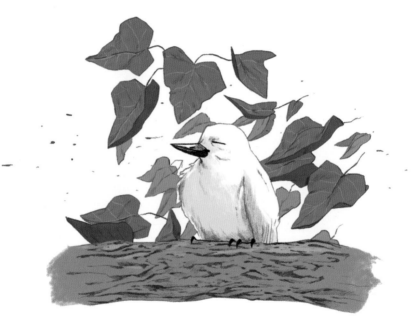

* brought to Hawaii by ancient Polynesians

And the most attractive person you
can imagine is nearby saying,

"Come on, let's go beneath the waterfall."

"Okay," you say,

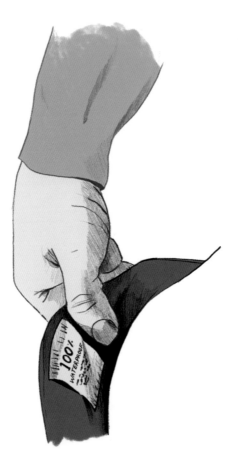

"these shorts are alright to get wet."

And after putting your wallet, cell phone,
and rental car keys on a rock, you join them.

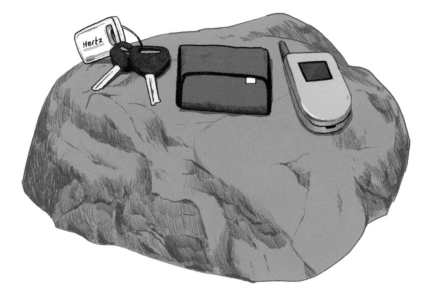

Have you stood beneath a waterfall before?
It actually kind of hurts.

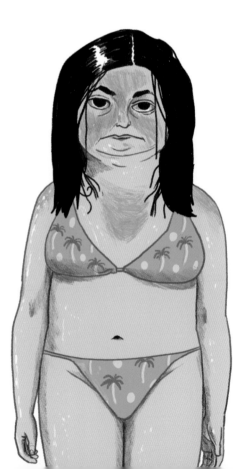

If you look up, it's like getting sprayed
by a Super Soaker in the eye.

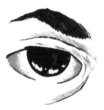
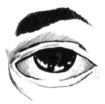

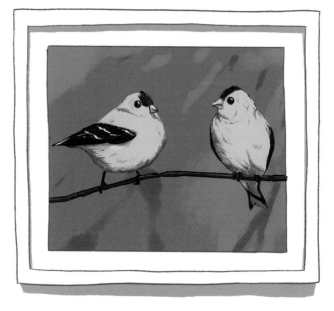

Sorry, that's not relaxing to think about...
How's the bathtub doing?

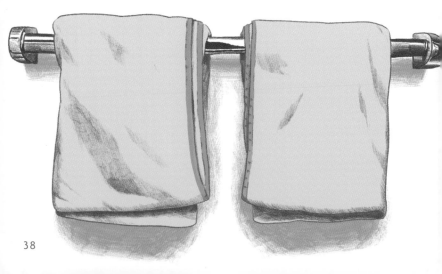

Oh nice, about a third of the way full...

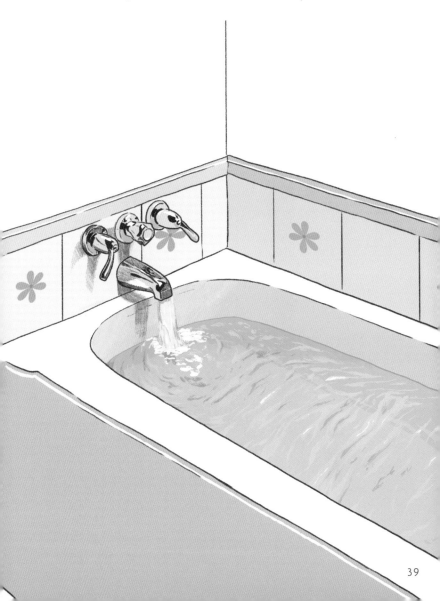

Do you mind if I ask- what's the longest you've ever hid in the bathroom before?

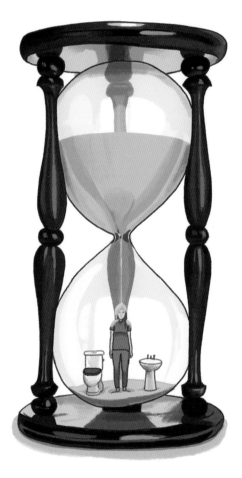

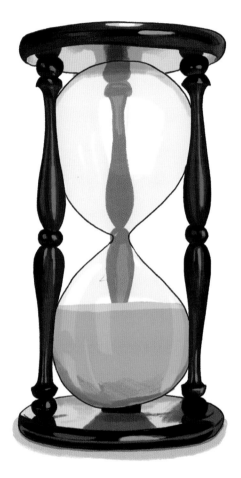

Woah, that's a while.

Me?

Maybe an hour but I can't remember the specifics.

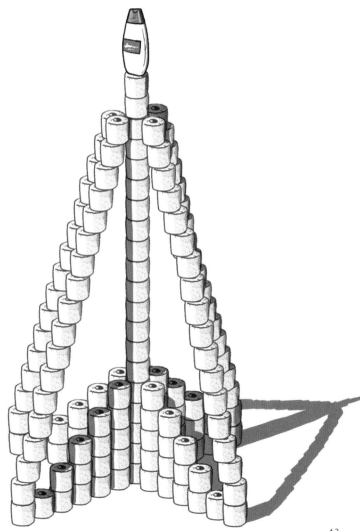

But I do remember the first time I realized
that I could take sanctuary in the bathroom.

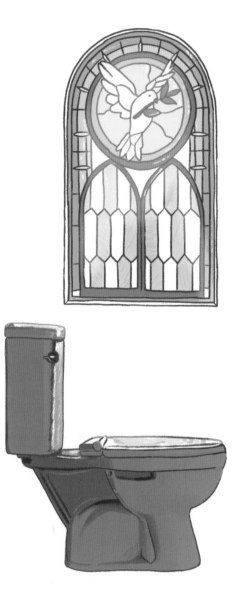

I was 12 years old at my cousin Maria's wedding
and discovered that if I just stayed in there,
I wouldn't have to dance with my aunt.

She's a heavy drinker and really knows
how to swing a chubby kid around.

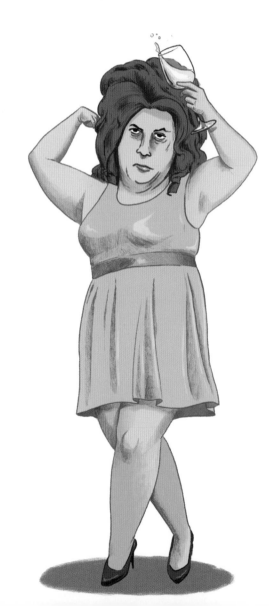

Sorry to my aunt but I can't be the only one who's ever hidden in the bathroom to avoid a dance.

Weddings...

...maybe my fear of marriage comes from
the fact that I understand the seriousness of it.

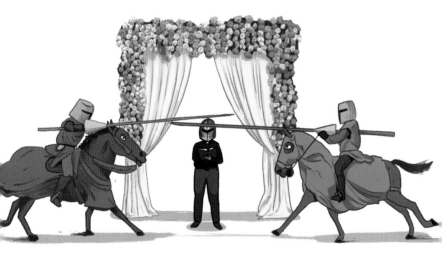

It's a lot of time to spend with someone.

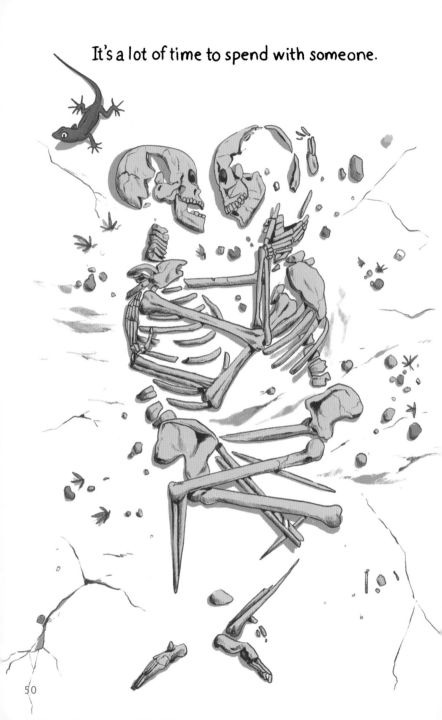

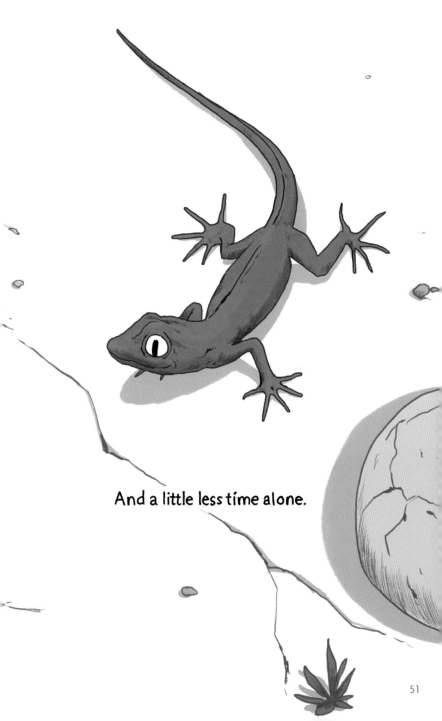

And a little less time alone.

N
W
S
Yes, sharing intimacy and affection with another person is good.
Isn't this beautiful?

But a bit of quiet solitude is pretty good too.

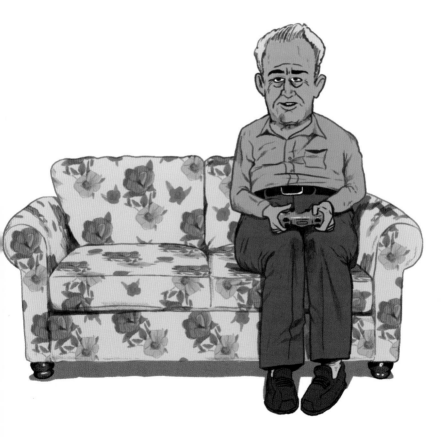

In a moment like this,

wouldn't it be nice

OUT
HUN

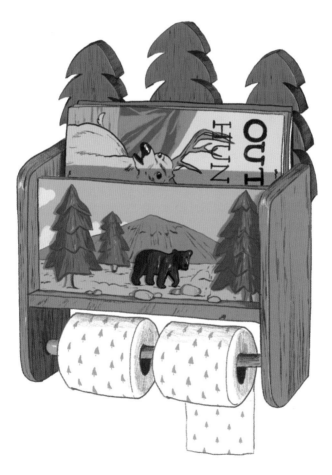

to just wander into the woods for a while?

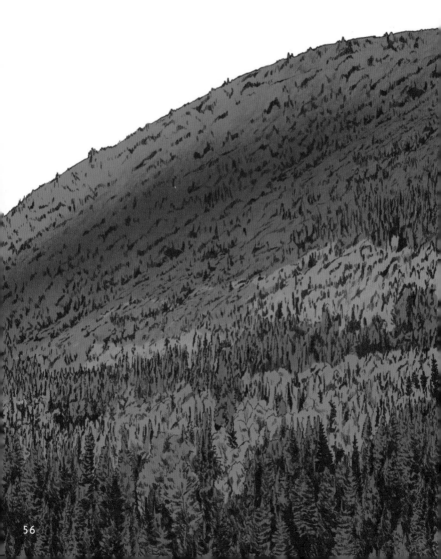

Move to Alaska and live in a cabin
you've built yourself?

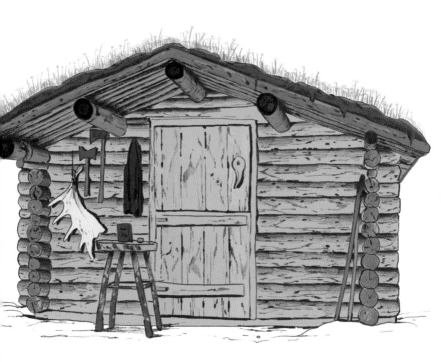

Like retired mechanic Richard Proenneke
notably did from 1968-1998?

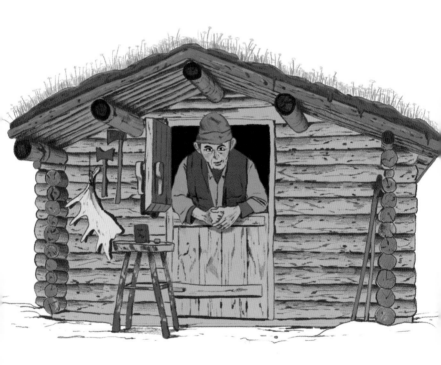

You could go out each morning like Richard
with your 16mm camera and film Dall sheep all day.

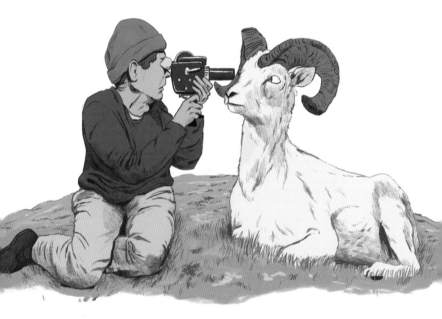

In the afternoon,
catch a trout and eat it for dinner.

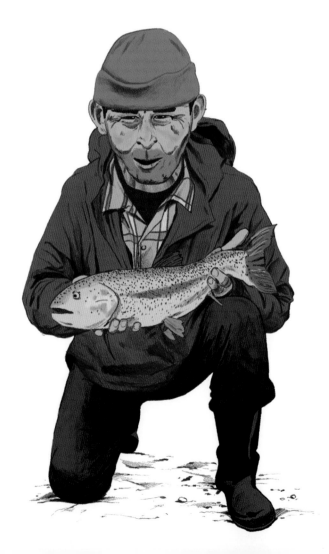

And then, in the evenings,
just stare at the fire until you're ready for bed.

Without a single person around to interrupt your thoughts,
you could spend hours thinking about how good the trout tasted.

TROUT.

You could also become a monk...

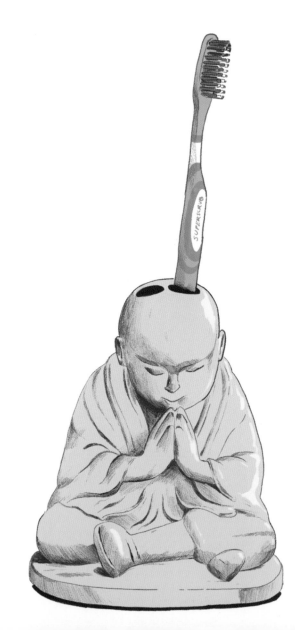

...you choose what kind.

Catholic monk
NI
ΦX
ΘΘ
KA'
ΦΠ
ΘΘ
TC
XX
TK
ΔΦ
XX
ΠΓ
Rare

But if you became a Buddhist monk,
you could perhaps reside at the Taung Kalat monastery,
atop a volcanic plug.

Not only would it be beautiful,
but through monastic living, you could develop
techniques to help you endure situations
like the one you're currently in.

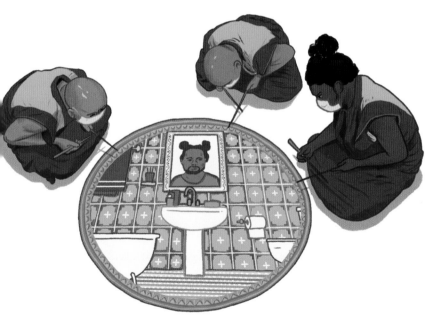

Though there's probably not enough time
for a spiritual transformation in this bathroom,
maybe we can at least try to put things into perspective.

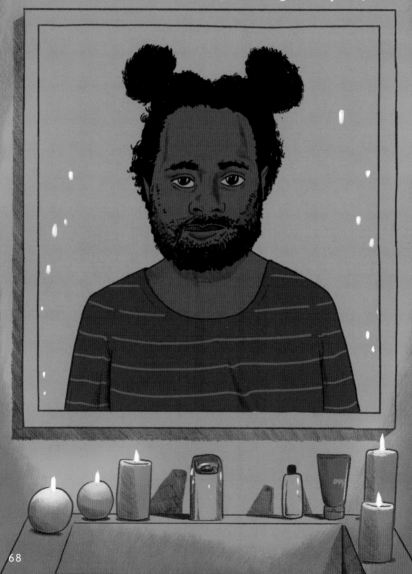

I mean, whatever's going on outside that door
can't be the worst thing that's ever happened to you.

If it is, you can turn to page 107.

But chances are you've been through worse.

For instance, you've passed the bar exam, you can listen to Shaun out there talk about CrossFit for 30 minutes.

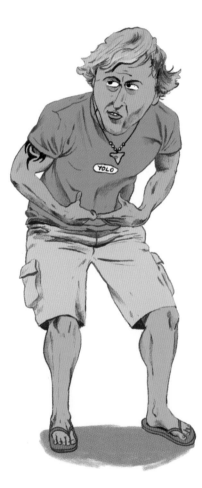

You've disappointed people before,
you can let the car salesman know that
despite the fact that your children go to school together,
you cannot afford to purchase a car out of guilt.

You've seen some terrible things as an emergency responder, you can watch the rest of the film without screaming every time E.T. comes onscreen.

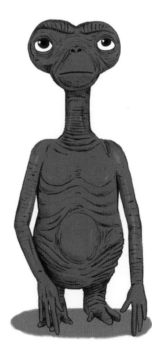

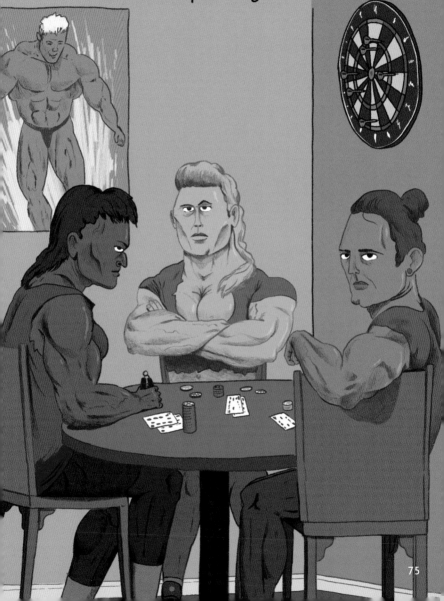

You've survived being thrown before,
you can go down there and say,
"Alright all you female bodybuilders, including my wife,
it's 2a.m. and poker night is over."

You've endured angry clients before, you can go out there and tell them you've lost all of their money investing in a new kind of trolley.

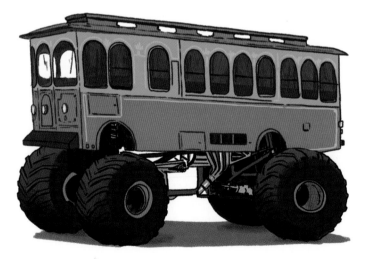

You're Jane Goodall,
you've lived in the jungle with chimpanzees for over 15 years,
you've written 25 books and made 7 films,
you're not sure why they asked you to participate
in the NBA Skills Competition,
but you can go out there and hold your own.

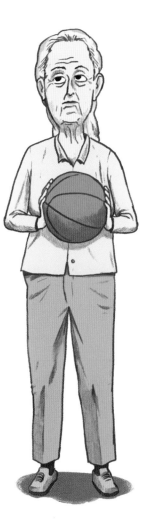

You've embarrassed yourself at parties before,
you can go out there and say, "Sorry, but it was me
who spilled the laundry detergent. I know it's inappropriate
to poke around someone's laundry room during a
holiday party but my former lawyer/ex-husband
was coming around the corner and I didn't expect to
run into him here. And while I was in there,
working up the confidence to engage with him,
I noticed this really interesting looking bottle—
a type of detergent I've never seen before—
and decided to take a look. The cap was loose
and you know what happened next.
I am sorry and will clean it up. And sorry to those
who slipped and hit their heads.

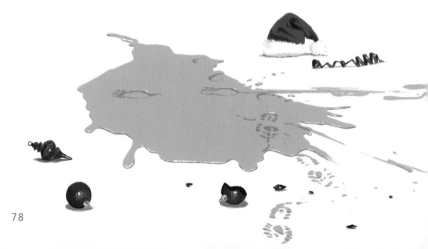

Anyhow...

BAND AID

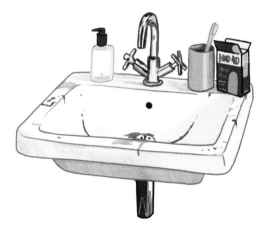

It's probably not possible to stay in this bathroom forever.
People will either think something bad happened
to you or they might just have to pee.

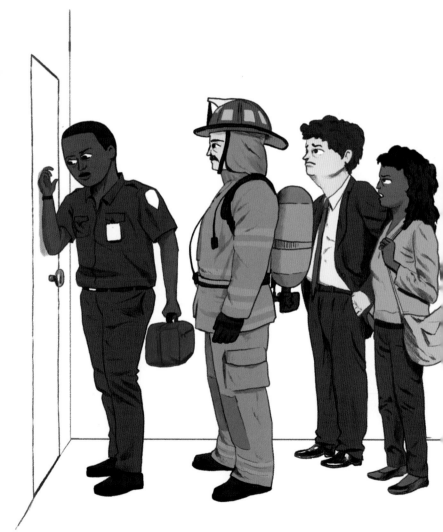

But by now, the bathtub should be full
and if you'd like, you can remove your clothes and get in.

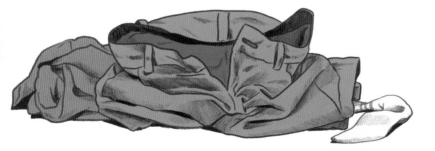

If you don't want to, that's ok too,
but wherever you are in the bathroom,
say this aloud to yourself:

I have good intentions.

I believe in myself.

I feel like I'm 22.

I have never had my heart broken.

I still trust the government.

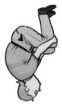

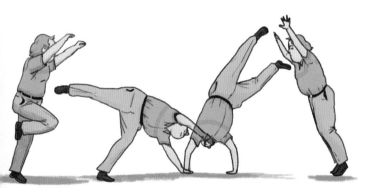

I am 3 inches taller.

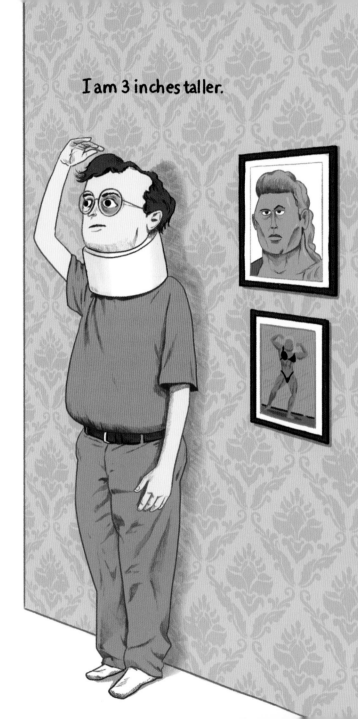

I can dunk every time.

There's no place I'd rather be but here.

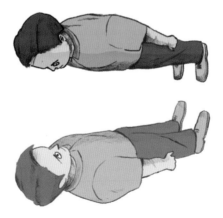

Oh, how previous generations of humans wish they had the wealth of antibiotics available to them that I have to me.

What I own is enough
and this applies to my hairline as well.

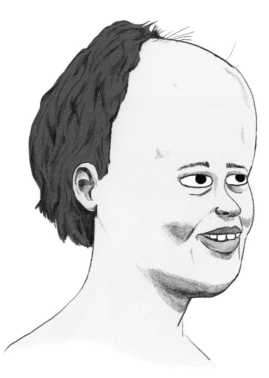

I can hit a fastball and absorb every unkindness.

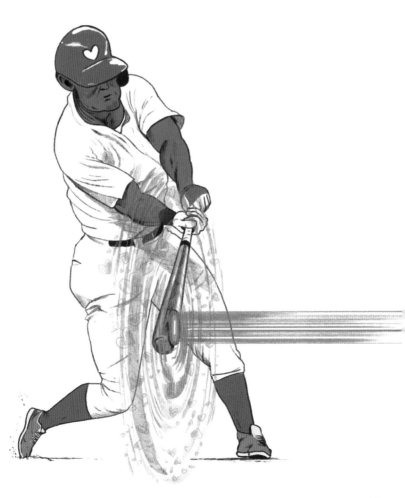

I will mow the in —   between   strip of lawn
that's technically   my neighbor's.

I won't get angry when cut off in traffic and in fact, I will honk at them to let them know that it doesn't bother me at all.

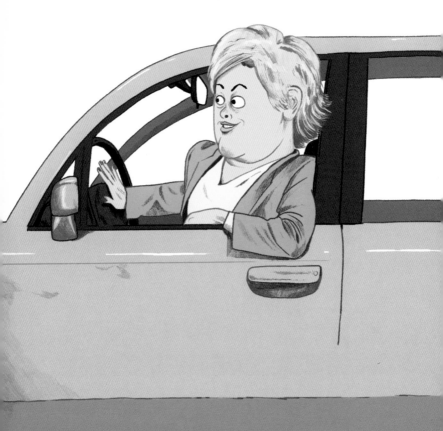

I will be honest except for in instances
where it might be unnecessarily hurtful,
in which case I will talk about lighthouse restoration.

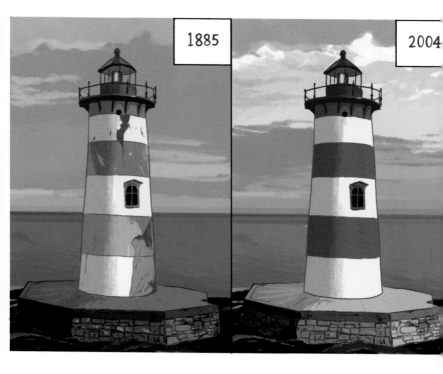

I will not prompt conversations about my dreams from last night or music festivals that I've attended.

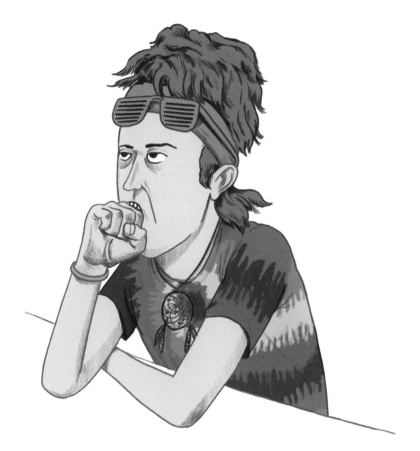

I did not leave the cooking gas on.

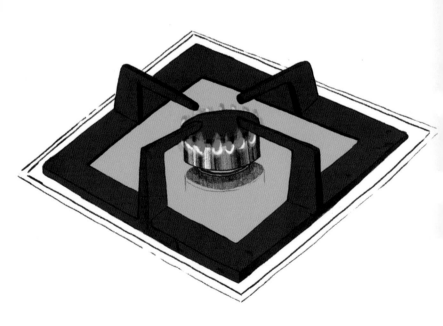

I did not leave the cooking gas on.

And maybe I should get married.

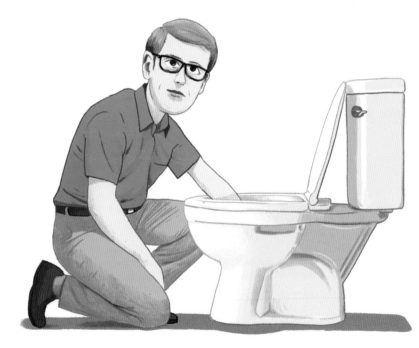

Maybe I should give it a shot.

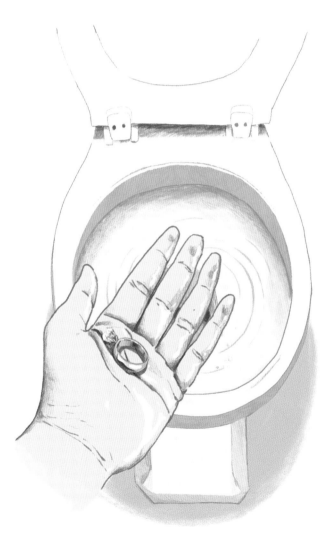

Time spent with another person is good.
Maybe even necessary.

And I did not leave the cooking gas on.

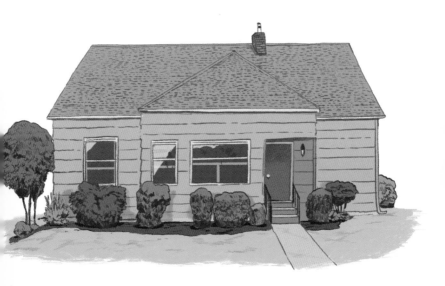

In summary, I will leave this room with the confidence of Donna Summer plus Dwayne Rock Johnson and everybody out there, including myself, will be "rocking their bodies."

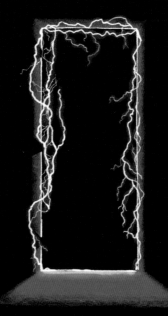

Heck yeah, this is good.
Let's go out there and if it doesn't go well,
I can *always* come back.

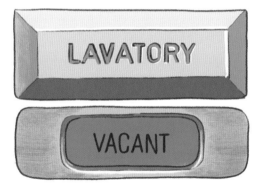

The bathroom will always be here for me.

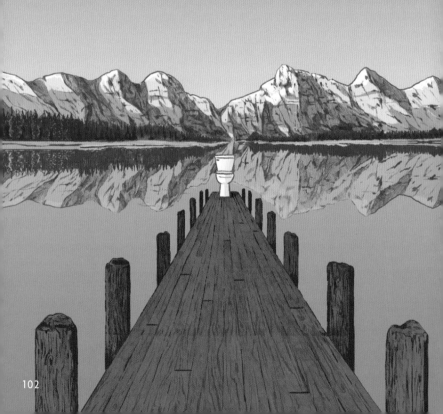

And if you are in the bathtub, dunk your head

and when you come up...

you are reborn,

with more confidence than you've ever had in your life.

And you can reenter the party naked and wet.

EPILOGUE

In case it'd help, I figured I'd include some conversation starters that have worked for me in the past. Hopefully they can help you too.

1. Do you believe in free will or fate?
   (Depending on their answer, you can drink their drink.)

2. You ever start a fire someplace you shouldn't?

3. Who ya think Frankenstein'd vote for?

4. What is the maximum amount of years you can hold on to anger?

5. What would you do if your daughter brought home a boyfriend who looked like Sméagol?

6. Do Kit Kats count as granola bars?

7. Woodwinds or brass?

8. When is the last time you just felt "good"?

9. Would you let them fling you into space?

10. Did you know that in 2018, the U.S. imported 22 billion dollars' worth of seafood?

11. Did you know that in 2017, the U.S. imported 21.5 billion dollars' worth of seafood?

12. And in 2016, it was 19.5 billion dollars' worth?

13. Here is the chart of the 5 years before that:

2015–$18.8 billion
2014–$20.2 billion
2013–$18 billion
2012–$16.7 billion
2011–$16.6 billion

So what do you think is responsible for the increased demand for shrimp?

14. What's the last book you lied about reading?

15. Do you keep a flashlight next to your bed? Why not?

16. What do you think popular music would sound like if Roy Orbison were still alive?

17. Isn't it a shame that we live in a time where it's no longer appropriate to name a bar 'Bazonks'?

18. How far do you think you could throw a baseball without using your fingers?

19. In my opinion, we will know our society is on the right track when they allow elderly people to sit at the front of the airplanes instead of the rich.

20. What's your favorite type of little guy*?
*bug

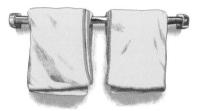

*This book is dedicated to anyone who
has ever used a bathroom*

ACKNOWLEDGMENTS

Thank you to the regulars at the *Dan Joe Charles Show* and the audience of *The Blueberry Tour* who helped decide what material was worth putting into the book.

Also, Vincent Tsui, Matt Owensby, Dan Licata, the NY Distilling Co., Adult Swim, Oliva Gerke, Lisa Mierke, and Meredith Miller.

Also, Ali Fisher for her support and patience, Kristin Temple, Jeff LaSala, Steven Bucsok, Heather Saunders, Alexis Saarela, Libby Collins, Jennifer McClelland-Smith, Linda Quinton, Lucille Rettino, Fritz Foy, and Tom Doherty.

Also, Dabir Bulbar, Kathleen Neighbors, and to our families.

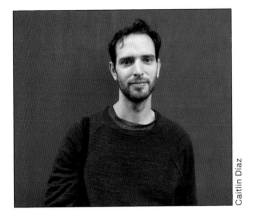

Caitlin Diaz

ABOUT THE ILLUSTRATOR

JOE BENNETT is an artist and filmmaker living in Pasadena. He's made original works for FX, FOX, MTV, Comedy Central, and Adult Swim.

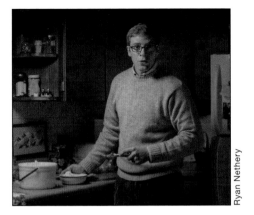

Ryan Nethery

ABOUT THE AUTHOR

JOE PERA is a stand-up comedian from Buffalo, New York now in New York, New York. He has performed stand-up on *Late Night with Seth Meyers* and *Conan,* guested on *The Late Show with Stephen Colbert,* and is the creator/writer/star of the Adult Swim series *Joe Pera Talks With You.*

You can find more of his work as well as stand-up dates at joepera.com

A BATHROOM BOOK FOR PEOPLE NOT POOPING OR PEEING BUT USING THE BATHROOM AS AN ESCAPE

Copyright © 2021 by Joseph Pera and Joseph Bennett

A Forge Book
Published by Tom Doherty Associates
120 Broadway
New York, NY 10271

www.tor-forge.com

Forge® is a registered trademark of Macmillan Publishing Group, LLC.

The Library of Congress Cataloging-in-Publication Data is available upon request.

ISBN 978-1-250-78269-4 (hardcover)
ISBN 978-1-250-78270-0 (ebook)

Our books may be purchased in bulk for promotional, educational, or business use. Please contact your local bookseller or the Macmillan Corporate and Premium Sales Department at 1-800-221-7945, extension 5442, or by email at MacmillanSpecialMarkets@macmillan.com.

First Edition: May 2021

Printed in China

0 9 8 7 6 5 4 3 2 1